Roger Doss

On Some Hash Functions: Constructing a randomized binary search tree and a hash table

GRIN Publishing

Bibliographic information published by the German National Library:

The German National Library lists this publication in the National Bibliography; detailed bibliographic data are available on the Internet at http://dnb.dnb.de .

Imprint:

Copyright © 2013 GRIN Verlag GmbH
Print and binding: Books on Demand GmbH, Norderstedt Germany
ISBN: 978-3-656-37505-0

This book at GRIN:

http://www.grin.com/en/e-book/209288/on-some-hash-functions-constructing-a-randomized-binary-search-tree-and

GRIN - Your knowledge has value

Since its foundation in 1998, GRIN has specialized in publishing academic texts by students, college teachers and other academics as e-book and printed book. The website www.grin.com is an ideal platform for presenting term papers, final papers, scientific essays, dissertations and specialist books.

Visit us on the internet:

http://www.grin.com/

http://www.facebook.com/grincom

http://www.twitter.com/grin_com

On Some Hash Functions
Dr. Roger G. Doss, PhD

Introduction

Hash functions are very important in Computer Science. A hash function maps an input key with a much larger set of possible values to an output key with a restricted set of possible values. Traditional use of hash functions are in the implementation of hash tables. A hash table is an array where values are stored based on the outputted key value from a hash function. This article will present several hash functions as well as their intended use in implementing a randomized binary search tree (BST) and a fast hash table. The hash functions are not designed for cryptographic security.

Hash Functions

The first hash function to be discussed is called **hash3** in the code that references it. It is the third version of a function originally conceived as an experiment to see how many unique values can be produced given unique string input. After experimenting with two other versions, this version was settled upon. The experiments utilized writing C++ code to extract unique words from sample text files and hashing them with this function. After the words were hashed, the integer output was compared for uniqueness. In the experiment, we observed that for the 10,000 unique words[1] that were hashed, the function produced 9962 unique integer values[2] which is an improvement over the previous version which had 8494 unique integer values. The function is:

```
unsigned hash3(const char *str)
{
    unsigned val_tab[] = {0x6938d27,
                0x929dd4cb,
                0xd05819e3,
                0xb2a035fb,
                0xa3988717};
    unsigned val  = val_tab[*str % 5];
    for(; *str; str++) {
        val += *str;
        if(val % 2) {
            val <<= 1;
        } else {
            val >>= 1;
        }
        val ^= val_tab[*str % 5];
    }
    return val;
}
unsigned inthash(unsigned val)
{
    char str[1024]={0};
    sprintf(str," %d",val);
    return hash3(str);
```

}
Notice that **inthash** is a function that uses hash3 to hash integers while hash3 is designed to hash strings. The design of hash3 focuses on a prime number set of random or pseudo-random integers stored in an array called val_tab which are used as exclusive or values while the string is iterated. The array may be larger than the illustrated five values provided the size is prime. The selection of which exclusive or value to use is based on the value of the character at that pass modulo the total number of possible values. There are prime many of these values such that the value is relatively prime to the character. The rest of the function accumulates the string value and shifts left or right one bit at each pass based on whether or not the value is odd at that pass.

The second hash function is a combination of hash functions based on existing hash functions. Instead of resolving collisions simply by using a collision list, the function uses four hash functions to look up a symbol. If all four functions fail to retrieve the data requests, the function then uses a collision list to find the data before ultimately giving up. The function is:

```
T &operator[](char *key) throw (int)
{    if(!key) {
        throw (-1);
    }
    int numeric = get_numeric(key), start = numeric;
    if(t[numeric].key && !strcmp(t[numeric].key,key)) {
        return t[numeric].t;
    }
    numeric = get_numeric_1(key);
    if(t[numeric].key && !strcmp(t[numeric].key,key)) {
        return t[numeric].t;
    }
    numeric = get_numeric_2(key);
    if(t[numeric].key && !strcmp(t[numeric].key,key)) {
        return t[numeric].t;
    }
    numeric = get_numeric_3(key);
    if(t[numeric].key && !strcmp(t[numeric].key,key)) {
        return t[numeric].t;
    }
    for(node<T> *n = t[numeric].next; n; n = n->next) {
        if(n && n->key && !strcmp(n->key,key)) {
            return n->t;
        }
    }
    throw (-1);
}
```

Where **t** is an array of class node containing a pointer to the data and a pointer to next such that each entry in the table is capable of having its own linked list. The above code shows how four hash functions are tried in an attempt to find the data with a matching key, and that if none of the look ups succeed, then the last attempt's linked list is checked; otherwise the function fails to retrieve the item. Insertion is similar, except the last step is not to search a linked list for an item; but to insert into a linked list:

```
    if(!t[numeric].next) {
        t[numeric].next = new node<T>(key,value);
        count++;
        return true;
    } else {
        node<T> *n = new node<T>(key,value);
        n->next = t[numeric].next;
        t[numeric].next = n;
        count++;
        return true;
    }
```

The four hash functions get_numeric* can be found here[3]. get_numeric is the sdbm hash function and get_numeric_1 is the djb2 function referenced in [5]. get_numeric_2 is the SAX hash function referenced in [6]. get_numeric_3 is the Boost hash function referenced in [4].

Data Structures

Randomized Binary Search Tree

The hash3 function was used to construct a randomized Binary Search Tree (rBST) and the get_numeric hash functions were used to construct a hash table. For rBST, the main data structure contains a class Value and pointers for left and right children as well as a pointer for next to construct a linked list. The linked list is needed for collision resolution. If there is a collision which occurs when two or more unique keys hash to the same value, the linked list is employed to store the data. Every node within the tree can have its own linked list as every node is possible to have the need for collision resolution. The left and right pointers allow implementation of the binary search tree in the usual way. The class Value contains to unsigned integer values, one for the result of the hash3 function applied to the key, and the other the original key value. For the sake of testing and without loss of generality, the Value class uses an original key which is also integer, but it can be of other types such as string or floating point. The core binary search tree node class is given in part by:

```
class BSTNode {
    Value value;
    BSTNode* left;
    BSTNode* right;
    BSTNode* next;
    ...
};
```

The heart of the rBST structure is the hash of the original value prior to insertion into the tree. This hash is intended to randomize the values and prevent values from being inserted that are simply ordered sequences. The ordered sequences produce runs in the data structure equivalent in complexity to linked lists and are therefore O(N). However, since most binary search trees use recursive logic, if the run is too long, it will likely lead to even worse performance in practice and possibly stack overflow and crash the program. The idea behind using a hash function is to keep the tree balanced as possible and at the same time, not spend time re-balancing the tree as would be the case in Red-Black and AVL trees. The key; however, is the hash function. The code for insertion requires that the class Value hash the original key which is done in its constructor and that this hash value is used inside the tree:

```
class Value {
  public:
  unsigned int  value; // Hash value.
  unsigned int rvalue; // Original value.
  Value()
    : value(0), rvalue(0)
  {
  }
  Value(int _value)
    : rvalue(_value)
  {
    value = inthash(_value);
  }
  ...
};
```

An important point is that collision resolution requires that the tree can not handle insertions, look-ups, and deletions entirely in the usual way. Insertion requires that there be a check to assert if there is a collision, then the to be inserted item is inserted in the correct tree node but on its linked list. This code is as follows:

```
bool BSTNode::add(Value value) {
    if (value.value == this->value.value) {
        // This is a collision.
        if(value.rvalue != this->value.rvalue) {
            if(!next) {
                next = new BSTNode(value);
            } else {
                BSTNode *ptr = new BSTNode(value);
                ptr->next = next;
                next = ptr;
            }
            return true;
        }
        return false;
    }
    else if (value.value < this->value.value) {
        if (left == NULL) {
            left = new BSTNode(value);
            return true;
        } else
            return left->add(value);
    } else if (value.value > this->value.value) {
        if (right == NULL) {
            right = new BSTNode(value);
            return true;
        } else
            return right->add(value);
    }
    return false;
}
```

Notice that collision occurs on insert when we have two hash values that are the same and the original values are different. In that case, there are two cases to handle, insertion into the linked list when the root list node is null and insertion into the linked list when the root list node is not null. The rest of the insertion algorithm is done in the usual way [7].

Similarly, look-ups require that if there is a collision, then the linked-list be scanned. The search still initially proceeds with a log(N) scan of the tree; however, the logic is looking for the hashed value. Once the node having this value is found, a check has to occur to see if the original value matches, otherwise, the value is possibly on the linked-list. If it is not found then, the value is not in the tree. The code is:

```
bool BSTNode::search(Value value) {
    if (value.value == this->value.value) {
        if(value.rvalue != this->value.rvalue) {
            BSTNode *ptr = next;
            while(ptr) {
                if(ptr->value.rvalue == value.rvalue) {
                    return true;
                }
                ptr = ptr->next;
            }
            return false;
        }
        return true;
    }
    else if (value.value < this->value.value) {
        if (left == NULL) {
            return false;
        }
        else
            return left->search(value);
    } else if (value.value > this->value.value) {
        if (right == NULL) {
            return false;
        }
        else
            return right->search(value);
    }
    return false;
}
```

Notice that as in the case for insertion, the condition for finding a collision is that the node first have a match on the hash value, but that node's original value does not match the one be searched. In that case, if there is a linked-list associated with the node, it is scanned. If there is a match on the list, in this implementation, the value of true is returned otherwise false. The rest of the code is the usual BST logic [7].

Deletion is slightly more complicated. The code can not simply delete a node as there may be a linked-list attached. There are several cases which can be grouped in a high level as a node having a linked-list and a node not having a linked-list. In the latter, this deletion is done in the usual way. However, in the former, there are two sub-cases. The first one is when the tree node itself is to be deleted, and the second case, is when the node is on the linked-list. If the tree node is to be deleted, then its value is swapped with the linked-list root value and the deletion actually occurs on the linked-list root node. In the case where we are to delete a node from the linked-list, a scan must first occur to find the list node to be deleted. This can occur at the root of the linked-list or somewhere in the body. If it as at the root, the root is deleted and a new root replaces it. Otherwise, if it is in the body of the linked-list, then the internal node is deleted. The code is as follows:

```
BSTNode* BSTNode::remove(Value value, BSTNode *parent) {

    if (value.value < this->value.value) {
        if (left != NULL)
            return left->remove(value, this);
        else
            return NULL;
    } else if (value.value > this->value.value) {
        if (right != NULL)
            return right->remove(value, this);
        else
            return NULL;
    } else {
        // Collisions are handled here.
        if (this->value.rvalue == value.rvalue && next) {
            // We are the node to be removed and we have
            // a linked list associated with this node.
            // Take the value from the list, and swap,
            // then delete the list root.
            this->value = next->value;
            BSTNode *ptr = next;
            next = next->next;
            delete ptr;
            return NULL;
        } else if(this->value.rvalue != value.rvalue && next) {
            // We are not the node to be removed and we
            // have a linked list associated with this node.
            BSTNode *ptr = next, *prev = next;
            bool found = false;
            while(ptr) {
                if(ptr->value.rvalue == value.rvalue) {
                    found = true;
                    if(prev == ptr) {
                        // Delete at root.
                        if(!ptr->next) {
                            // No other nodes on the list.
                            delete ptr;
                            next = NULL;
                            return NULL;
                        } else {
                            // At least one other node on the list.
                            next = next->next;
                            delete ptr;
                            return NULL;
                        }
```

```
            } else {
                // Delete a list node.
                prev->next = ptr->next;
                delete ptr;
                return NULL;
            }
        }
        prev = ptr;
        ptr  = ptr->next;
    }
    if(!found) {
        // Node was not found.
    }
    return NULL;
}
// Normal deletion otherwise.
if (left != NULL && right != NULL) {
    // This is the case where we are the parent of
    // a left and right subtree.
    this->value = right->minValue();
    return right->remove(this->value, this);
} else if (parent->left == this) {
    // We are the left subtree.
    parent->left = (left != NULL) ? left : right;
    return this;
} else if (parent->right == this) {
    // We are the right subtree.
    parent->right = (left != NULL) ? left : right;
    return this;
}
    }
}
```

Hash Table

The get_numeric hash functions where applied to implement a hash table. The main contribution of the hash table is its use of multiple hashing functions prior to using the collision list for collision resolution. Traditional hash tables tend to use double hashing or collision list as a resolution method [8], in this hash table implementation the combination of the two was used in addition to utilizing more than two hash functions before finally using the collision list. The class definition is as follows:

```
template<class T>
class table {
  template<class S>
  class node {
    friend class table;
    char *key;
    S     t;
    node<S> *next;
    public:
```

```cpp
    node()
      : key(0),
        t(0),
        next(0)
    {
    }
    node(char *_key, S _t)
      : key(strdup(_key)),
        t(_t),
        next(0)
    {
    }
    ~node()
    {
      if(key) {
        free(key);
      }
    }
    void add(char *_key, S _t)
    {
      key = strdup(_key);
      t = _t;
    }
    void clear()
    {
      if(key) {
        free(key);
      }
      key = 0;
      t = 0;
    }
    bool operator==(const node<S> &obj)
    {
      if(obj.key && key && !strcmp(obj.key,key) && obj.t == t) {
        return true;
      }
      if(!obj.key && !key && obj.key == key && obj.t == t) {
        return true;
      }
      return false;
    }
    bool operator!=(const node<S> &obj)
    {
      return !operator==(obj);
    }
};

node<T> *t;
int size, count;

public:
// static const node<T> no_pos;
```

```cpp
    static node<T> no_pos;

    table(int _size)
      : size(_size),
        count(0)
    {
            t = new node<T>[size];
    }
    ~table()
    {
        for(int i = 0; i < size; i++) {
            t[i].clear();
        }
        delete[] t;
    }
    ...
}; // class table

template<class T>
table<T>::node<T> table<T>::no_pos;
```

The table contains an internal node class and both are C++ templates. The node class has a
node<S> *next pointer for constructing a singly linked-list. In the table class, an array of node class is
created as the hash table and allows for the construction of a list for every possible position in the table.
The look-up operation the aforementioned: **T &operator[](char *key) throw (int).** The insertion routine
follows a similar design:

```cpp
bool set(char *key, T value)
{
    if(!key) {
      return false;
    }
    int numeric = get_numeric(key), start = numeric;
    if(!t[numeric].key) {
      t[numeric].add(key,value);
      count++;
      return true;
    }
    numeric = get_numeric_1(key);
    if(!t[numeric].key) {
      t[numeric].add(key,value);
      count++;
      return true;
    }
    numeric = get_numeric_2(key);
    if(!t[numeric].key) {
      t[numeric].add(key,value);
      count++;
      return true;
    }
    numeric = get_numeric_3(key);
```

```
    if(!t[numeric].key) {
       t[numeric].add(key,value);
       count++;
       return true;
    }
    if(!t[numeric].next) {
       t[numeric].next = new node<T>(key,value);
       count++;
       return true;
    } else {
       node<T> *n = new node<T>(key,value);
       n->next = t[numeric].next;
       t[numeric].next = n;
       count++;
       return true;
    }
    return false;
}
```

The insertion tries up to four hash functions to find a slot within the table, and if it was still not successful, the code then uses the last slot as a linked-list node and inserts the new value on that list. It follows then, that deletion is:

```
void del(char *key)
{
    // Clear the underlying node.
    node<T> &n = get_node(key);
    if(n != no_pos) {
       n.clear();
       count--;
    }
}
```

There are some design considerations regarding deletion. In the above code, the node is simply cleared assuring that it will not reappear in a look-up operation. However, if its a linked-list node, the node should be freed otherwise it is possible that the table uses excessive memory. An alternative design could have the linked-list insertion logic first search for a node prior to allocating a new node for insertion on to the list. In this implementation, since get_node has to do a potentially O(N) search of the collision list to return the node, it is better to free the node in the proper way at that time and return. The get_node code to handle deletion at the collision list is:

```
    ...
    node<T> *ptr = t[numeric].next, *prev = ptr;
    while(ptr) {
      if(ptr->key && !strcmp(ptr->key,key)) {
        if(ptr == prev) {
          // Delete at the root.
          if(!ptr->next) {
             delete ptr;
             t[numeric].next = NULL;
```

```
    } else {
        t[numeric].next = ptr->next;
        delete ptr;
    }
    } else {
    // Delete regular list node.
    prev->next = ptr->next;
        delete ptr;
    }
    }
    prev = ptr;
    ptr = ptr->next;
}
return no_pos;
```

Note that in this design the code returns an empty node **no_pos** which is checked later on in the deletion method.

Performance

The performance of the randomized Binary Search Tree (rBST) was measured in comparison to the std::map and std::unordered_map of the STL on Linux Fedora 16. The test consisted of 10000000 or ten million insertions, look-ups, and deletions of sequential integer values in the three containers. Timings were recorded prior to the start of the insertions, and after the deletions, then the difference was computed to determine elapsed time for the three operations per container. The output in seconds of the performance test where the code was compiled without optimization was:

rBST 88.000000
STL std::unordered_map 32.000000
STL std::map 102.000000

The performance with -O3 optimization yielded a different output:

rBST 67.000000
unordered_map 24.000000
std::map 60.000000

The performance with randomized input, likely to be indicative of real-world usage was:

rBST 69.000000
unordered_map 31.000000
std::map 70.000000

Clearly, the randomized BST is at times faster or on order of the std::map but not the std::unordered_map which is much faster than both. The, randomized BST is a useful data structure as its logic is much easier to understand than that of the red-black tree based and widely used std::map.

The performance of the hash table was measured in comparison to the std::map and std::unordered_map of the STL on Linux Fedora 16. The test consisted of 20000000 or twenty million insertions, look-ups, and deletions of sequential integer values in the three containers. Timings were recorded prior to the start of the insertions, and after the deletions, then the difference was computed to determine elapsed time for the three operations per container. The output in seconds of the performance test compiled without optimization was:

hash table 28.000000
STL std::unordered_map 70.000000
STL std::map 224.000000

The performance with -O3 optimization yielded a similar output:

hash table 21.000000
STL std::unordered_map 57.000000
STL std::map 126.000000

The performance of std::unordered_map improved by creating a larger hash table on initialization, but was still slower than our hash table. Creating the std::unordered_map as:

unordered_map<string, int> test_map1(20000003);

Where 20000003 is prime improved that container's performance to 44 seconds. The performance with randomized input, likely to be indicative of real-world usage ,was the same as the performance with the non-random input. Clearly, the slowest of the three containers is the STL std::map likely due to its need to order the data. This is followed by the STL std::unordered_map. The fastest was the hash table described herein.

Conclusion

The rBST data structure is a modified Binary Search Tree whose performance is inline with std::map; however, it has a much easier to understand implementation. The complexity of the rBST structure comes from having to hash the input keys and handle collisions while maintaining a vanilla BST structure. Perhaps better hash functions can be used in the future to improve performance.

The hash table designed herein was faster than std::unordered_map and std::map for the test that was performed. The table can hopefully serve as a basis for future implementations. Future work includes considerations for making the hash table concurrent. For a copy of the source code, which is provided under the terms and conditions of the GNU Public License (GPL), see [9].

References

[1] Price, E. (2012). 10000 Word List – MIT. Retrieved April 30, 2012 from
http://www.mit.edu/~ecprice/wordlist.10000

[2] Doss, R. (2012). hash_test.cc. Retrieved May 6, 2012 from
http://www.rdoss.com/papers/hash/hash_test.cc.html

[3] Doss, R. (2012). table.h. Retrieved May 6, 2012 from
http://www.rdoss.com/papers/hash/table.h.html

[4] Boost hash. Retrieved May 6, 2012 from
http://www.boost.org/doc/libs/1_37_0/doc/html/hash/reference.html#header.boost.functional.hash_hpp

[5] Yigit, O. (2012). Hash Functions. Retrieved May 6, 2012 from
http://www.cse.yorku.ca/~oz/hash.html

[6] Gunn, T. (2010). SAX was designed for hashing strings. Retrieved May 6, 2012 from
http://www.daniweb.com/software-development/cpp/threads/231987/string-hash-function

[7] Binary Search Tree . Retrieved May 6, 2012 from
http://www.algolist.net/Data_structures/Binary_search_tree

[8] Cormen, T.H., Leiserson, C. E., Rivest, R. L., & Stein, C. (2009). *Introduction to algorithms*. Cambridge, Massachusetts: The MIT Press.

[9] Doss, R. (2012). hash source. Retrieved February 6, 2013 from
http://www.rdoss.com/papers/hash/hash_src.tar.gz